The No-Stress
Your First Six Figures

NO PRESSURE PRESSURE WASHING

MATT JACKSON

Copyright © 2023 by Matt Jackson

All rights reserved. No part of this publication may be reproduced, distributed, or transmitted in any form or by any means, including photocopying, recording, or other electronic or mechanical methods, without the prior written permission of the publisher, except in the case of brief quotations embodied in critical reviews and certain other noncommercial uses permitted by copyright law.

Book Design by Matt Jackson

CONTENTS

Introduction: About Me 4
CHAPTER 1: Why You Need This Book 7
CHAPTER 2: The Right Mindset 9
CHAPTER 3: Where Do You Start?
            How about a Why… 11
CHAPTER 4: Your WHY Becomes Your Brand 13
CHAPTER 5: Choosing Your Ideal Customer 15
CHAPTER 6: Market Analysis 17
CHAPTER 7: Marketing 101 20
CHAPTER 8: Sales 101 24
CHAPTER 9: Getting Your Business Set Up 29
CHAPTER 10: Build Your Online Presence 32
CHAPTER 11: Google 35
CHAPTER 12: Traditional Marketing 37
CHAPTER 13: Your Book of Business 39
CHAPTER 14: Know Your Numbers 41
CHAPTER 15: Pricing Strategy 43
CHAPTER 16: Sales Goals 45
CHAPTER 17: Equipment 101 47
CHAPTER 18: Employees 49
CHAPTER 19: Standard Operating Procedures...... 51
CHAPTER 20: Replication 53
CHAPTER 21: Reputation 56
CHAPTER 22: Where do you go now? 58

INTRODUCTION: About Me

I'm Matt...but everyone else calls me The Driveway Guy. I probably have a similar story to a lot of you. I grew up being outside and playing competitive sports. I played baseball until I graduated college and then had to join the "real world" where I landed jobs in corporate sales.

Being a competitive guy I needed an avenue to channel my drive to better myself. I noticed quickly that the normal career path of getting a degree, working for the man, and hustling for someone else was NOT for me. After job hopping and selling in multiple industries from B2B industrial sales, car sales to tech sales I decided enough was enough and I was going to start my own thing.

At that time I had a ton of "book knowledge" from voraciously reading books, listening to podcasts and channeling all my angst of **not knowing who I wanted to be into consuming every piece of information I thought would help me become the person I thought I needed to be.** Surprisingly it didn't work...I was dead set on reinventing the wheel and not looking at what I had the means to do at the time. I didn't have capital to invest in something big or a highly sought after skill.

I finally asked myself what I knew that would be a translatable skill to make a business. Funny enough I had a pressure washer, a 3.5 GPM Honda GX390 that I used in college to clean my parents and neighbors driveways for spending money in the summers. I decided to make a Facebook page and start my company and the rest was history...well not so much.

I started the page in 2017 but like many of you second guessed myself and didn't do anything for another year. I was so full of ideas that I had become paralyzed by over analysis. I continued working my day job and lived the life of quiet desperation pushing my dream down like I had before. Until one day I got a call from a random number asking me if I pressure washed and how much I would I charge?

As fate would have it I decided this is the time to go all in. If I'm not pushing this and people are reaching out to me. Imagine if I actually took ACTION and applied myself. From then on I side hustled myself into outgrowing my corporate income and decided to make the jump of faith to be full time in June of 2020 during COVID.

Leaning into the same faith I had putting myself out there to quitting my day job to scale to multiple trucks is one of the most rewarding feelings as we are near-ing a million dollars in revenue since the jump. It's not about money it's about proving who you are to YOUR-SELF. Money gives you the fuel to keep going! The fuel to chase opportunity and see how much you can do in this world.

I promise you there is no better job than working for yourself. The pressure washing business model is a great business to jump into with a great community. If you are reading this and on the fence about it you just need to lean into that little voice inside that tells you to DO IT.

The Early Days..   Free Used Equipment/Summer Hustle

College Baseball

Computer Printed Marketing Fliers

CHAPTER 1:
WHY YOU NEED THIS BOOK

Did you know the pressure washing industry amounts to over a billion dollars a year? Yes we look around and see that everyone has jumped into starting a professional cleaning business but I assure you...there is plenty of work to go around! Pressure washing is a fantastic starter business because it's a cash based business where you can start with a lot of HUSTLE and not a lot of money. It is one of the easier businesses I have been in that has a great upside POTENTIAL.

So what is stopping you from making six to seven figures spraying water? If you are like me, when I first started it was easy to be stuck in analysis paralysis (where you consume too much information you don't know where to start). Information without application is useless and we can get stuck in obsessively consuming YouTube videos of internet gurus or reading comments on Facebook of unvetted people giving their opinions.

The longer you are in the pressure washing space. The more you see the personalities, gurus, equipment sales guys who push their product as the only answer. You start to see that there is no PERFECT product, method or GURU to follow. At the end of the day what makes you successful boils down to how much VALUE you provide to your community.

Don't worry -- we aren't going to leave you hanging on "provide value" is the " key to success" we will break down what that means to us. What we learned from years in the industry and almost a million dollars in revenue. This book will cut through the noise of the 30,000 ft view of things and give you some real applications that will instantly get you on the right path to creating your own successful local pressure washing business. Buckle up and get ready for your first few steps!

Avoid the traps of chasing the "secret" and buckle up for the journey.

CHAPTER 2:
THE RIGHT MINDSET

Before we start picking out business names, ordering equipment and trying to find clients it's very important to have a solid understanding of the right mindset to have. Unlike a "job" your business becomes an extension of YOU. So your level of success in business usually correlates to the level of VALUE you as a person provide to your community. One of my favorite quotes, "Your Attitude is Your Altitude" will dictate your level of success.

I see so many people getting into business without the right mindset and they end up failing. We must shift our mindset from a consumer or "taker" to being of service and a "giver". Business is a lot like planting a seed and waiting for it to grow into a tree. If we don't pour into the seed with care and patience it will never sprout. We are not directly benefiting from all the effort as the tree grows but eventually it will bear fruit and we then see the reward.

We must have an abundance mindset to start a business in order to give and serve others without seeing an immediate reward. The easiest way around this is to stop thinking conditionally about every interaction. I have re-framed my life around being a giver without holding expectations of an immediate return. Knowing the true return will come back multiplied down the road.

We must become someone of value, that translates into someone who is of a servant's heart and gives more than they receive in every transaction. Once we make this transition life has a way of giving us clues of our next path and opens doors to relationships that wouldn't be possible otherwise. This will raise your "Frame" or energy and attract people to you. Remember people don't care about what you DO, they care about how you make them FEEL.

CHAPTER 3:
WHERE DO YOU START? HOW ABOUT A WHY...

Congratulations! With the right mindset of being a go- getter and a giver it's time to get started on your business. But before we jump into the technical aspects like registering your LLC, getting insurance and proper licensing we need to figure out what our business represents.

Most companies set themselves up to fail before they start because they don't have a WHY behind them. They choose to jump right into the "technician" mode and don't create a brand and culture first. Remember we are here to build an irresistible business that attracts an endless supply of clients and employees down the road. We want our business to hold a weight in the community that it "sells itself" with reviews, referrals and raving fans.

The key is building something bigger than yourself. Your WHY should be something personal that has a deeper meaning to you and your community than you are just here to make some money. Remember money FOLLOWS value. If you try and force money before value you will chase it away. You are much better off spending more time in the beginning setting up your business to align with the right why for you than jumping into it trying to hustle and sell a low value business.

When I started my business I chose a name based on an authentic emotion and built that story into my brand. I noticed everyone around me was either a larger "corporate" company or chose a generic name like XYZ pressure washing. The WHY I had was the energy of hard work, humility and serving my local community as a neighbor. If you follow my business today my entire marketing is based on that emotion. Matt The Driveway Guy -- "Professional Quality From a Friendly Neighbor". We deliver exceptional results, over communicate, and have a great customer experience. More importantly my team has a CULTURE to follow.

CHAPTER 4:
YOUR WHY BECOMES YOUR BRAND

You have probably heard major companies stress the importance of their "brand". Most companies don't really have a compelling "brand" that is memorable, emotional, and separates themselves from other businesses in their industry. Think of the major companies. Apple, Amazon, Coca-Cola vs. Microsoft, Walmart, Pepsi they are all very similar companies but they invoke a different "emotion" or image when thought of.

Before you start picking out a name for your company, decide what kind of feeling people will have when they hear about you. Do you want to brand yourself as something unique and authentic to YOU. Or choose to be more of a generic brand that will blend in with others in your industry. I specifically chose a personal brand for my business to cut through the noise of generic companies in my area. I chose to tap into an authentic energy when creating Matt The Driveway Guy that resonated with people in my small town.

Remember when people Zig you want to Zag. The key to adding value to yourself is to stand out in the marketplace and you do so by your brand that showcases your WHY. Instead of jumping to create a generic name, think of something memorable and personal to YOU that resonates with your ideal customer. I work with homeowners and small businesses in a small southern town so my brand resonates as the "friendly neighbor" who does a great job with southern hospitality.

The simplicity of "just call Matt" allowed my brand to quickly spread in my area since I target the emotion of selling myself and my story. This also allows me to stem into other services based on the reputation I have built without having to recreate a new company if I chose XYZ Pressure Washing.

Remember business is an extension of your identity. So why not make it and extension of you. Pick a brand that aligns with your values and sell yourself from the heart and naturally attract clients to you!

Instead of Copying The Masses

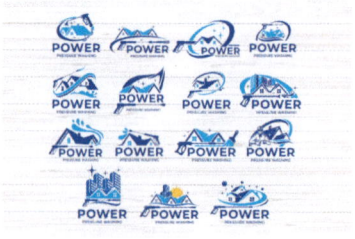

Use Your WHY to Stand Out

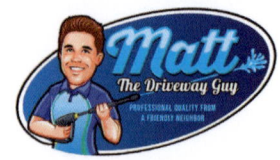

CHAPTER 5:
CHOOSING YOUR IDEAL CUSTOMER

One of the MOST important things to do before you start creating your business is figure out exactly WHO is your ideal customer. Remember we start our own businesses to WORK for US. We aren't aimlessly taking on work or working for people that don't allow us to grow to our best selves.

We have a few options with Pressure Washing. We can work Commercial or Residential or specialize in certain services that we enjoy doing and can maximize profitability. I have personally enjoyed working with residential clients as my brand aligns better with homeowners and the marketing avenues I excel in. Word of mouth is easier to spread in residential areas, you get paid the same day in cash and if you are lucky the homeowner will let you clean their business too!

Once you decide what service you want to focus on you need to create a customer avatar of your perfect customer. The avatar is going to be as specific as you can be for that person. For example --I want to target 35-55 year old married female homeowners in middle to upper middle class families that value hiring someone "professional" that they can trust and have a good reputation in the community. Let's call this avatar "Ashley". For the residential market the woman is usually the decision maker of the home and approves the services done to the house. So we want to be the best possible FIT for her!

We want to be as specific as we can when coming up with our customer avatar because we are going to model our marketing and branding for that person. We want to speak directly to "Ashley" so our message resonates with her and there is no reason she won't use us. Our goal is to be as personal as we can be to form a connection that will lead to our IDEAL customer for life and a raving fan who will refer us to everyone they know!

By having clarity of your IDEAL customer and using that to perfect your message you will SEPARATE yourself from your competition.

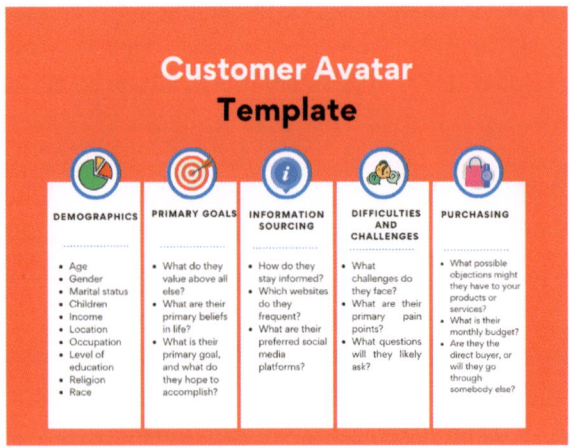

CHAPTER 6:
MARKET ANALYSIS

Understanding your market is one of the most important things when it comes to marketing and selling yourself. I see many companies who do a fantastic job advertising but struggle because they aren't aware of their surroundings. As a business owner we need to be an expert at our market and competition. We should know who the top players are in the area, how they market, how much they charge and how they service customers.

Business isn't a static game where we have our head down plowing forward. Our success in marketing comes with understanding the MARKET around us. Before we create our brand we should research our competton to figure out how we can use our strengths to STAND out from our competition. We should study the best in our industry and figure out exactly what they do to be the best. You don't want to COPY them but you want to study and understand them. They got to that point because they are the best at what they do. You want to MODEL what works for them and put your SPIN on it.

You NEVER want to copy someone else's business because you will come off as a counterfeit to the market. We want to use them as influence and put our own spin on how we can make it BETTER for our IDEAL customer. Remember we aren't going after ALL customers...we are going after our IDEAL customer!

When I was creating my company I took pieces I liked from the well known HVAC guys who dominated locally. They put their faces on their vehicle and went with the personal brand approach that seemed to work really well in my town. I modeled another company's social media postings (this company was a digital marketing company out of Texas) and put my spin on that. I took a little bit from here and there that resonated with my authentic self so I could create my natural voice (what your customers FEEL about your brand).

My area has always been a great market for Pressure Washing but it's always SATURATED. So I needed to find ways to position myself DIFFERENTLY than the huge companies and generic owner operators. If you don't take the time to identify your competitors and come up with a game plan to position yourself differently you will struggle to get ahead.

Here at Matt The Driveway Guy we are constantly adapting and pivoting to stay fresh in the eyes of our market. What worked last year doesn't work the same today. So it's important to keep your pulse on the market and be flexible to stay unique. We heavily reinvest in our branding via new uniforms, wrapped trucks, new videos, we always want to showcase NEWNESS because in today's age people gravitate towards the best new thing.

When we started we didn't have employees / fancy trucks and equipment so we were authentic with

MARKET ANALYSIS

where we were in business and sold it well! Now we have trucks, employees and a large marketing budget.

The takeaway here is to always be aware of your surroundings and think of how you can improve where you fit in your market. In order to be a leader in your space you have to CREATE and not COPY. You should always be studying successful businesses both in and out of your market to stay ahead of the competition. Remember if you are repeating what you do year over year you will have FLAT numbers.

CHAPTER 7:
MARKETING 101

Marketing is the MOST important thing in any business. Now what exactly do we mean by marketing? I like to think marketing is the activity or business of promoting products or services. In order to "Sell" a customer we first need a "lead" which is where marketing comes into play. You can be the best at sales but if you suck at marketing you will never get ahead! Our main objective when marketing is to be SEEN and DIFFERENT than our competition. Think of marketing as your BAIT. If you are fishing for work you must always have fresh bait on the line.

There is a famous saying in marketing called the 4 P's...Product, Price, Place and Promotion. You need to think of your business in terms of how your SERVICE fits into that equation. We don't want to be broad when thinking about our business and how we FIT the demands of our customers. The main problem people face in business is coming off generic and unoriginal. In highly competitive markets like pressure washing that is a way to find yourself lost in the sea of fish or losing jobs based on price. Because your customers don't find value in your brand you sell off price alone!

Here is a basic example of the 4 P's with Matt The Driveway Guy. The 4 P's is a solid framework to use as an exercise to get clarity of your marketing strategy and brand position. The 4 P's allow us to identify what makes our **Product** unique, where to **Price** our product, where we need to **Place** our product to get in front of the right customers and how we need to **Promote** our product. While this exercise may be simple it's important to get a basic idea of how you want to MARKET your company.

Once we map out the 4 P's with our business we can get into the fun stuff of actually creating and actively running campaigns! But remember it's vital to have the RIGHT marketing before we waste money advertising.

4 P's Exercise

Product:
What is your product?
Residential Pressure Washing In Greenville, SC
What does your product do? Does your product meet an unfilled need or provide a novel experience?
We Provide The Best Customer Experience, Overdeliver on value (BIG BRANDED/ Always do more), Kind and communicate
Who is Your Products target audience?
Homeowners in Greenville, SC
Price:
What is the price range of your products competitors?

We fit in the middle of the market. We overdeliver on VALUE so word of mouth and repeat business drives growth

What is the price range of your target audience?

Our audience has enough discretionary income to justify and average service of $500 every 18 months to spend

What price is too high for your audience? What price is too low?

Too high would be +700 too low is below -300

What price best fits your target market?

We seek to attract the customer avatar of working professionals with around a $500 budget for a basic service.

Place:

Where will you sell your product?

We largely sell our product online via social media, Google, and word of mouth.

Where does your target audience shop?

Our target audience likes to use social media and Google to find their service providers

What distribution channels are best to reach your target market?

Google, Facebook, Instagram, Local Journals

Promotion:

What is the best time to reach your target audience?

The best time is all the time. Since we use social media we use interruptive marketing to spark a demand on the customers timeline.

What marketing channels are most effective for your target audience?

Facebook/ Instagram, Google

What marketing messages would most resonate with your target audience?
We are professional and very well branded and care about the customer experience. This customer seeks the BEST
What advertising approaches are most persuasive to your target audience?
Professional Videos, Well done websites, Uniforms, wrapped trucks, High Google Reviews.

The 4 P's help guide you to think in the right direction with what you want your company to represent, who you want to attract, how you need to be priced in the marketplace, and how you reach those customers. During this time we recommend doing a lot of market research to better understand how you fit into the market.

Remember when you start you are never locked into a specific marketing strategy or brand. We personally always strive to evolve our brand to stay fresh.

CHAPTER 8:
SALES 101

Sales and marketing go together like peanut butter and jelly. Marketing is important but without closing those leads you into sales you will fail.

Marketing brings in the leads –which are customers interested in getting a service and the sales part is when you convert the lead to money.

A company's sales are measured in revenue and are the lifeblood of an organization. Without selling anything a business cannot afford to stay open and by that definition you have a costly hobby and not a business. If you are new to sales or aren't the best "people" person don't worry because sales is a process that can easily be learned.

There are millions of books out there on sales with different philosophies all claiming to get you rich. Remember – **what you say means less than how you make someone feel.** Selling is all about making someone feel GOOD where they give you money. Instead of studying what to SAY, focus on creating a relationship with your customer that's based on trust.

People buy from people who they know, like and trust so the way to win over prospects is to get rapport (trust) and ask the right open ended questions. Our goal is to get them talking about their needs. Why did they reach out to you? What are they needing cleaned? Try and find the deeper reasons behind what they want done.

The more we know about the prospect the easier it will be for us to provide them with a solution. Remember we are there to FIX a problem they have. We aren't a burden...we have to make an emotional connection with the prospect to gain trust and the more value we provide them the more money we make.

While there is no script you should follow, it's important to follow a few steps to make sure you consistently ask the right questions. Let's call this the "10 Tips To A Sale".

10 Tips To A Sale

1. Make sure to take charge of the conversation but do so with a positive attitude. We want to get the customer to follow our lead as we bring them through this process. Remember first impressions are very important! Our goal isn't to give a price, it's about getting them to warm up and trust us so they can answer our questions!

2. Get all the information needed up front. Full name, phone #Email and address. You want to know the scope if you are to wash the entire project in the back of your mind. Think of this as your GAMEPLAN.

3. Find out how they heard of you? Where they found your information will dictate a lot on how you are PRE FRAMED (what they think of you). If you come

on word of mouth, Google Reviews, Following on Social media you have a lot of VALUE already. Vs if It's a COLD lead (randomly calling without knowing you) you will need to build value.

4. We quote a LOT over the phone and via text. We also want to align with how the customer wants to communicate—for lower ticket jobs under $1000 we find it easy to close over the phone or via text. For higher ticket and more complex projects like commercial or bigger sealing projects we always quote in person because it requires more emotion to close the deal.

5. Once we have all the information and find out what they need to have cleaned, we want to know why they need it done, what their timeline is, have they had any experience in the past with competitors etc. Some people request services they think they need, not services we can HELP them with. So this is where we uncover unknown needs.

6. When we present the numbers we always give them options. If we present someone with one number their option is YES or NO. If we give people multiple options they can make a decision while still purchasing from us. Usually the objection of "shopping" doesn't come from price as much as wanting another option to choose. We always give GOOD, BETTER, BEST (this is where we quote the other services we offer) solutions with discounts to incentivise a buying decision. Our job is not to force a decision, it's to allow them to pick and feel in control!

7. When presenting the quote we always lead them to a path of least resistance. We don't allow them to tell us if they want it or not. We let them know the next available appointment time. Remember this is what we do everyday this isn't personal so we shouldn't feel scared or nervous of whether or not they say yes. This is where maintaining control of the Sale is vital. If you let them lead here they can back out or try and negotiate pricing.

8. Negotiation? We get people try and negotiate with us on price. We always suggest adding on another service at a discounted rate vs subtracting from the quote. When people ask if we negotiate we always suggest bringing in a neighbor for a group rate. Remember we don't want to "LOSE" we want to Give more value and not LOWER ourselves. We can throw in a sidewalk/ or bring in a next door neighbor and do a bulk rate. That allows us to max out our timeslot and everyone wins.

9. Over Communicaiton. The name of this game is to be as responsive and helpful as possible. We want to get the lead, give them pricing options and present them with a time to book as fast as we can. Most companies struggle with communication so half the battle is being the first to respond!

10. Over Deliver. If you overdeliver, price is never an issue. Give them the best customer experience from the quote request to the review request and you will have loyal raving fans that use you year over year. Remember it's not about just chasing new business but building the referral network

and the repeats! The best sales tactic is great word of mouth!

AIDA is a great framework as you lead the prospect to the close!

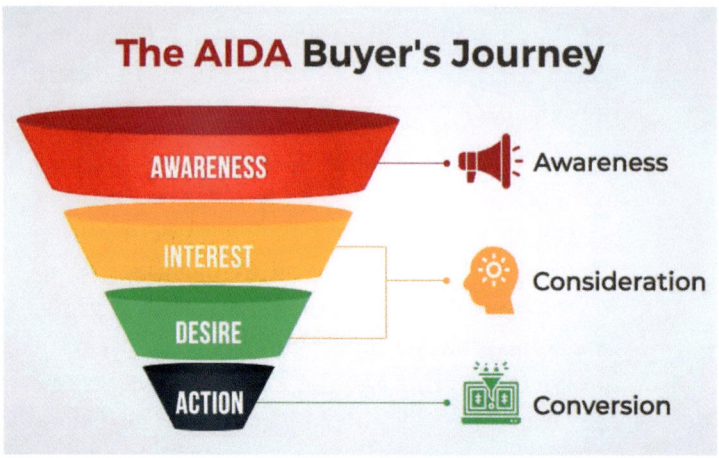

CHAPTER 9:
GETTING YOUR BUSINESS SET UP

When you start your business you are having to wear ALL the hats. This can be confusing when you first start out because oftentimes we are good at one thing and not the rest. When I started I knew the sales and marketing but I had to figure out the Operations. I had to figure out what all running a business consisted of.

How hard could it be? I just get jobs and pressure wash and collect money right? When I started I didn't have an EIN, LLC, Business Accounts, Business Cards, Insurance. I was the $99 guy because I didn't have the knowledge or money to jump in with both feet first. While I was able to start that way I don't recommend it.

One of the first things you should do after you decide upon a name is to get an LLC. You can pay your state legislator and register it online for a small fee. This allows you to create a shield around you from a personal liability standpoint. You want your business to be separate from your personal life. From there register your business with an EIN (Employer Identification Number) think of this as your TAX ID. You can also find this by googling and pulling it from the IRS website. There are many legal services that will do this for you for a fee if you are concerned but I was able to complete it all myself.

Once you get the EIN and LLC you can then open a business bank account. Usually the bank can offer you a business credit card through them as well. Until your business is about 2 years old you will have everything tied to your personal credit. Because of this your credit limit will usually be very small. You will need to pay down the statements often to avoid having too much "credit" utilization lowering your personal credit score.

You can also get a DUNS # which is a business credit rating system. This helps you grow your business credit score to position yourself for financing and business loans. The goal of business is to hold all the assets and liabilities under the LLC vs your personal. That way down the road you can be in multiple separate entities without damaging your personal scores!

Pro tip: Make sure you get your business accounts and credit started early that way you can offload your personal credit to your business. After 2 years I moved my business cards to American Express and got to enjoy the benefits of points and business financing options that help with growth!

Once you get your business accounts set up I highly recommend getting QuickBooks and a CRM. We use HouseCall Pro as it allows us to manage our customer database, collect payments, schedule jobs, get reviews, and run the day to day. We would not be able to operate today without HCP.

Quickbooks is your accounting software to help you manage your books. The sooner you track all your numbers the better off you are for tax season and you can accurately grow your business. These apps both allow you to track your vehicle mileage that comes in handy as well during tax time to get the deductions!

For insurance I highly recommend finding someone local to help you out. There are plenty of websites that offer you insurance but usually those are priced at a premium due to convenience. Usually a good broker can connect with other great services that can benefit your business as you want to offload as much work as you can onto hiring out. The mindset of a business owner becomes finding the right person to do the job vs doing it all yourself.

When you make the decision to set up your business you are giving up control and taking on more oversight.

CHAPTER 10:
BUILD YOUR ONLINE PRESENCE

There are 2 types of marketing strategies. Online and Offline. Somepeople refer to offline as traditional marketing. That is flyers, yardsigns, door hangers, clip flyers, EDDM, print media ect. When you first start out you have many options of getting your name out there. For me I didn't have a lot of money so I chose the online route.

I created Facebook, Instagram, Reddit, NextDoor, Google, Yelp page and whatever "other" free posting sites were out there and started posting about my business. Since I had more time than money I just plugged away getting my name out there. This allowed me to work my day job and do this during downtime and evenings. I was able to book my first jobs off of free postings that turned into money I could put into paid advertising.

When you use online marketing make sure you are speaking with the correct voice for the platform. If you are on Facebook–you want the post to be well received on Facebook. Use memes, videos, and satisfying content to spark interest. I see people post boring copy paste style low effort posts on social media and complain that it doesn't get attention!

Work your power base..the beauty of social media is you can share your information with your friends, their friends, family and neighbors. For a home service based business that is your CLIENT. Make sure you join all the neighborhood community groups and post content that separates you from everyone else. **Remember don't post what you DO post WHY you do it.**

Social media is a visual platform where people go to escape. We want to please their eyes with satisfying pictures and videos and entertain them. Everytime you post you have to think what can I do to capture people's 3 seconds of attention who are scrolling through for entertainment.

If you are unsure on content I highly recommend following our page Matt The Driveway Guy and modeling it. Don't copy and paste but go through and see what we do and put your spin on it. When I was coming up, people loved my Memes. Again people d**on't care what you do, they care how you make them FEEL.** I have made six figures off of memes.

Once you build up your social media platforms I highly recommend investing in paid ads. You want to make sure your content works first so if you can get high quality videos made and have high organic engagement those tend to work really well on ads. This will help your brand awareness in your market.

Once you get some cash flow you need to invest in a professional website that is designed well and has on page SEO and a form to collect leads. I use 180sites.com for my website and have been very happy with them.

They provide a visually appealing website with a great funnel that drives leads to my phone.

You don't want to be cheap with a website. Rule of thumb being cheap will cost you more in the long run! After all, if it's cheap to you, imagine how cheap you look to your customers...

Your online presence is your real time digital word of mouth. How you decide to look online will be one of the biggest deciding factors in your business success!

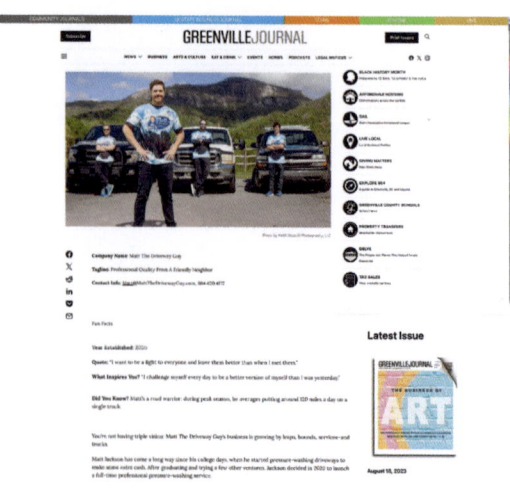

CHAPTER 11:
GOOGLE

Google is the holy grail of search engines and can make or break your business depending on where you rank with them. It's very important to optimize your website to rank on google and it's usually best to hire someone for SEO who can stay on top of the ever changing algorithms.

SEO is great but Google My Business or what's now Maps/ Business Profile is a must to be listed on Google. You need to sign your business up and verify it via Google to get a listing on their map packs. This allows people to give you reviews and you to show up for valuable keywords. A google lead is a great lead because it's a customer ready to buy!

You need to spend time setting up your Google business profile and upload pictures to it, keep content uploaded and work on getting as many reviews as possible. I have been able to rank myself very high on Google due to strategically and consistently staying on top of posting and getting reviews. This has given me so much local authority in my market that allows me to grow.

If you have money to invest I highly recommend Google Ads. You select the keyword and locations of where you serve and pay for clicks that turn into leads. Correctly running Google Ads will make or break your business growth. We probably do 150k a year just off Google ads at an ad spend of 15k.

We rank #1 For pressure washing search terms organically

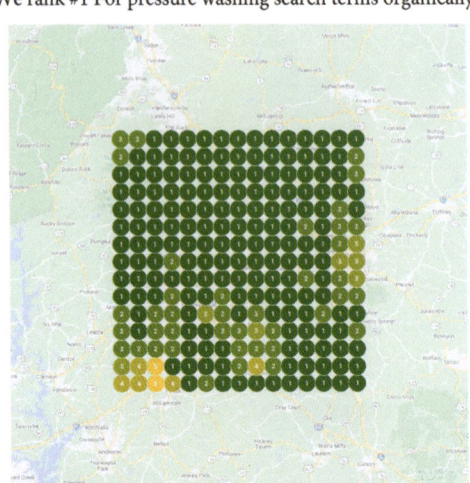

We automate 5 Star Reviews to have the #2 highest number of reviews in our area!

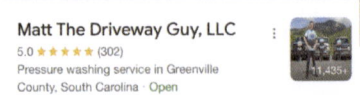

We strategically use Google Ads to get over 2 million impressions and 35k website clicks!

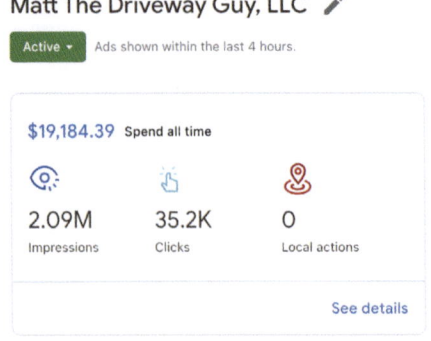

CHAPTER 12: TRADITIONAL MARKETING

Online marketing is my go too but that doesn't mean you can't make a ton of money on traditional marketing. Honestly you really need to do both to maximize your return. While I would love to automate marketing and have everything handled on a computer that isn't the reality of life.

Social media paints one view of the world that doesn't always reflect reality. Yard signs, flyers, door knocking, print media can produce massive amounts of business. Feet on the street works because people are being people to people. Not watching each other behind a computer screen. Nothing beats having an in person interaction so if you have the ability to be face to face you increase your odds of closing higher tickets more often.

One of the biggest companies in my area and the nation has grown their business off of clip flyers in driveways. So don't feel like you have to pick one area of marketing to be successful. The truth is do a good job in as many areas as you can and you will average out great!

We are the leading company on social media in my area and our google ranks high too. I will do EDDM campaigns and buy a page in the local print journal yearly and will still get people who have only heard me through the traditional media we send out.

We have 7 million impressions online in an area of 1 million but people still are only hearing about us from a journal piece or flier or seeing our guys in their neighborhood? Hmmm could it mean that social media doesn't always hit your entire target market? Yes! We are all about leading the way and reinvesting in our online presence but sending fliers and having our wrapped trucks gets us customers who have never seen us online.

The point is don't get too wrapped up in metrics on a screen and ignore the reality that most people out there probably haven't heard of you because they aren't in the echo chamber online. As we are scaling I am having to widen the net of bait we throw to catch fish from a different pond.

One other thing to note too. It takes multiple touches (times our marketing is seen) for people to get into a buying decision (with cold traffic). We can hit them with online ads, they see our fliers at home, they see our trucks on the road, they see us working in their neighborhood and finally they reach out. You need to always be top of mind so when they are ready to make a decision you are their go to!

CHAPTER 13: YOUR BOOK OF BUSINESS

As soon as you get your first customer you need to get all of their information and store it for later. The Value of a CRM is building your customer base with first names, last names, emails, phone numbers, addresses and everything you need to know their lifetime value. As we grow year over year we amass a large amount of repeat business that if we don't "farm" will lose that business to someone else.

I am able to send emails to my customer base to keep them updated on the growth of my business, monthly specials as well as send them follow ups 6 months and a year after their last cleaning. We want to be able to remind people to simply get back on our schedule so they don't have to actively think of it. That helps us keep consistency as well as they have the value add of a clean home without thinking too much.

Don't be reactive with your book of business. That data is powerful. You can export your customer list and track where your market is the hottest. I refer to this as a HEAT MAP. What neighborhoods and cities do you do the most work in? That way you can strategically target those spots to try and sell more houses in that neighborhood.

Your book of business is also a HOT list of customers to sell new services you offer. As we grow we are expanding into higher ticket services such as roof cleaning, sealing, paver sanding. We have converted $400 house washes to $8,000 paver sanding and sealing jobs to the same customer. Find the low hanging fruit and keep serving your customers by educating them on all your service offerings.

You want to fight the urge to be one and done with a customer. The longer you are in business the more your focus should be on maintaining your base and sifting through raising your average ticket prices. We want to over deliver the best service to our BEST IDEAL customers.

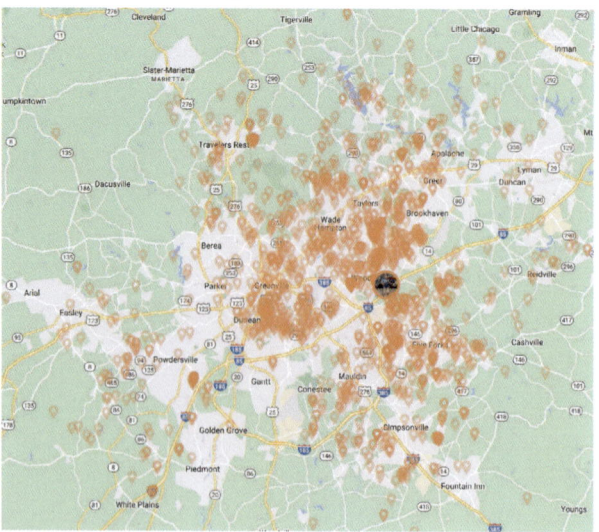

It is vital to farm your customers to create repeats and referrals!

CHAPTER 14:
KNOW YOUR NUMBERS

One of the hardest things about running a business is knowing your numbers. Now what does that mean? We need to be as "legitimate" as we can and track everything coming in and out. Many business owners over inflate their numbers whether it be intentional or not. Everyone chases the "Top line" revenue but doesn't factor the total cost of doing business which is the "net".

The sooner you get your numbers in check the easier it is to manage your business and understand the trends. Businesses fail due to cash flow problems. If we can understand the sales curves we can maximize our investments to get the best return on our money. We also can be prepared for the down months where we need to have a savings account in place.

If you aren't a numbers person you don't have to worry. Quickbooks is a great tool to help you manage and reconcile your revenue and expenses that you can sync to your business cards and accounts. Once you get rules in place it will run on autopilot.

You want to classify your expenses based upon categories and percentages allocations. As you grow your business you adjust the percentages allocated to each category. So when someone asks how much do i spend on X that number is tied to a percentage of production. By doing everything based on a percentage you know how much you can afford to spend. Knowing your numbers is vital to understanding your marketing schedule so you can maximize the busy season.

You can plan your business based upon your own personal goals and have a CPA help you fill in the blanks based on what you are trying to get out of it. Remember we get taxed on net income so the IRS encourages us to keep reinvesting to grow our business. You should be very aware of where you stand numbers wise, have your tax strategy in mind as well so you can prepare for the slow season, tax season or have enough capital to reinvest in new equipment.

Actively Track in a CRM

Report in QuickBooks

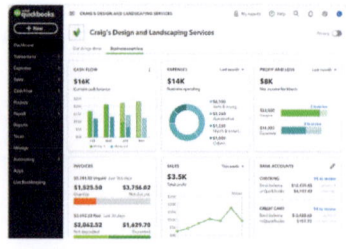

CHAPTER 15:
PRICING STRATEGY

Pricing is a major component in your business and marketing. If you remember that **Price** was part of the 4 P's of Marketing. Your pricing strategy must be aligned with your customer avatar and your value to the market.

If you are priced too low you will not have enough profitability to grow into a higher value business. The same applies if you are priced too high and don't have enough market value to close enough work to make money. When you are new or in a growth phase of business you want to close as much business as you can so your closing percentage is higher. But the focus is to maximize your day.

If you are a brand new business owner operator you want to make a minimum of $1000 a day as a goal. That is a great starting point where you aren't too high or too low and it's an easy number to replicate to hit your monthly and yearly goals.

When I first started I wanted to make 100k. It's simple math at this point if we can do 100 days at 1000, that's the math. If you work in a climate where there is no winter you could do that on the weekends! If you want to do that in half the time you just multiply your day rate by 2X.

Once you get busy to the point that you are making at least $150 an hour and staying busy you can raise your prices. You shouldn't be closing everything because if you do that means you are priced cheaper than the value you are providing. We close around 70% for residential now. However when we first started we were closing as much as we could to stay busy.

Know your worth and put a value on your time. As long as we are making $150+ an hour we usually are ok with the pricing. Remember it's better to not be the highest in town and stay busy and MAKE MORE than be the highest priced guy making half the revenue. Raising your price comes with raising value which comes with TIME!

Pricing Strategy Matrix

	Low Quality	High Quality
Low Price	Economy	Penetration
High Price	Price Skimming	Premium

CHAPTER 16:
SALES GOALS

When we set goals in our business it's important that we have a clear actionable GOAL to get there. Say our goal is 150k a year...we start by breaking the year down into months. We would need an average of 12k a month in revenue to hit that goal. Some months we will do less and other months we will do more. If in January we may do 6k but if we do 18k in June that av-erages out to 12 so we are still on pace.

We need to understand our seasons to put an accu-rate goal on the month. We call this the sales curve. Our busy season starts in March and goes until early July. We have to plan our sales to MAX out those months to really move the needle to hit our yearly revenue goals. We have a fall season that isn't as strong so we have to have a game plan for that as well.

Once you get a year of numbers under your belt you can find out what works to best maximize your sales goals. Big goals are great because oftentimes people undershoot and hit their low goals. However on the flip side we want a goal that we have a good chance of stretching to hit.

We want to set SMART GOALS: That means Specific, Measurable, Actionable, Relevant and Time Bound. Remember if we don't TRACK we will never HIT our goals so make sure even if you are off target you stay consistent.

SMART GOALS

- **Specific** — What *exactly* are you trying to achieve?
- **Measurable** — How will you know when you've achieved it?
- **Attainable** — Is it genuinely possible to achieve it?
- **Relevant** — Does it contribute to your agency's revenue growth?
- **Time-bound** — When do you want to achieve this by?

CHAPTER 17:
EQUIPMENT 101

Now that we have gone through the business basics, marketing and sales planning it's important to talk about equipment. While equipment is a necessity I find that it is often overhyped in our industry. Selling equipment is a huge business for vendors and the owner operator technician loves to get the best stuff. But having the most expensive equipment wont make you a dime unless you have your business optimized first.

I have run every type of set-up and currently have and love the efficiency of good equipment. We have run 3.5 GPM, 4 GPM, 5.5 GPM, 8 GPM, 12v, P40, open trailer, enclosed trailer and skids. Despite what loyalists say there is no one perfect machine. Each machine is a tool in an arsenal. We currently run a 2 truck set up with 8's and softwash pumps in the back of skids and a trailer unit and a 4gpm.

The 4 GPM is a great tool when we need to roll a machine out where we don't have access to park. The 8 GPM is our daily workhorse and the 12v and P40 come in handy on roofs and stucco. The majority of our money comes from downsteaming 8 GPMs and surface cleaning. The 8 GPMs put a ton of performance out for reliability. Remember we aren't trying to wash something once we are trying to run machines 8-10 hours a day 5-6 days a week. Money is made by consistency and not having downtime. Now that we have employees we have replicated the same set up on two trucks with skids.

The game plan is to systematize and keep it simple so that way everyone can be efficient with our equipment. We run 2 trucks that stick with soft washing and pressure washing and have another truck for more complex projects. The longer you are in business the less you are interested in the fads and more into the staple's that keep on running.

3.5 GPM

5.5 GPM

16 GPM

3 Trucks 36 GPM combined!

CHAPTER 18:
EMPLOYEES

Nobody wants to work anymore...it seems like this is common among business owners in today's climate. What we put out we attract–so it's vital that we take ownership of what we are attracting. If you are struggling to find employees, ask yourself "would I want to work for myself".

A lot of us get into business because we want control and the ability to do things our way. However you will get to a point where you either GROW or FAIL. We push so hard to grow our business from 0-100k+ that we become accustomed to that accelerated growth. Eventually we run into a point where we cannot grow and we become the hamstring of our own business.

Usually we get to the point where what was once our passion becomes our curse. We lose the spark and get overwhelmed by the workload. Unless we put our EGO aside and take on employees to help offload our work we will struggle.

I lasted two years full time with a helper before I HAD to get off the truck. I simply couldn't grow past the numbers I wanted to without killing myself. I personally had to GROW past the stage I was in when I was on the truck. I was hesitant at first and then I realized I was guarded based on my fears of failure.

I thought that I invested all this time and energy into something I can't afford to let go and have it crumble in the hands of someone else. In hindsight that was such a limited minded thought process. I had to think like a leader and not like an employee with scarcity. Once I began surrendering to the faith of trusting in my team my business really grew past my expectations.

I had to give ownership to my team and let them run without wasting my time micromanaging. I have to run things from a high level and steer the ship while the guys run the day to day. That means investing in the long term services, marketing and relationship building with other businesses in our area. It's easy to think small and stay on the truck being busy and not PRODUCTIVE. If you want to grow and have a LOT of fun. Surrendering your EGO and leaning into building a team around you that you empower will reward you with more reviews, tips, referrals and an overall better customer experience.

You aren't going to be pressure washing but you are going to be working ON the business which is a much more rewarding position. Sure mistakes happen and issues can multiply but with the right communication and culture you can scale your business and get off the truck!

CHAPTER 19:
STANDARD OPERATING PROCEDURES

The **key** to a successful business is **consistency** and **replication**. We need to figure out how to maximize our time with productivity. A huge learning lesson for most business owners is understanding the difference between busy and productive. Everything we do must be driving the needle forward or we are wasting our time. We need to audit our ideal day and write down what tasks are the most necessary to reach our business goals.

The things we do that drive our business forward are called operating procedures. It is very important to write down and "standardize" what our day looks like. If you have ever worked for another company, more times than not you had training and received a handout on their standard operating procedures. You need to treat your business the same way.

You want to create a guide on how to best run your day and follow it. This isn't meant to be rigid but you want to track your tasks and actions to figure out what works and what doesn't. It doesn't matter if it's just us or we have a team–the sooner we can standardize our business the more legitimate we become.

Remember we need to be consistent to hit our goals and will need processes to train employees that will **replicate** our output. If you don't have SOPs in place don't sweat it...get out a word document and write out everything you currently do in your business! You always want to work towards being an efficiency expert!

CHAPTER 20:
REPLICATION

I used to be a huge control freak in my business. My VALUE ADD to my market was my tight grasp on cleaning, quoting jobs, and being stuck IN my business.

"If you want to go fast go alone...if you want to go far go together"

The first couple years in business it's easy to do everything yourself. You can work 12-18 hours a day 6 or 7 days a week and chase the thrill of growing. However If you are any good at what you are doing you will quickly run into your limits. I gave it my all for 2 years as an ower operator before I was tired of plateuaing out at around the 180-200k mark. I was wide open chasing the seasonal swings doing it all solo only to realize if i wanted to pass a certain threshold I would have to get OFF the TRUCK.

I had spent so much time focusing on building my brand, pushing marketing and driving my business forward only to become the biggest hamstring of my business. If I was truly wanting to reach my potential in this business I had to fire myself from wearing all the hats and learn to delegate. To my surprise the hardest thing the hardest thing about hiring was in my head.

I simply ran facebook ads/ spoke with my current customer base and had great people come to me. We have 3 solid guys who were attracted to my business via my culture. So understand this. Branding not only attracts customers but your empoyees! Everyone complaining about the current labor market should look in the mirror. If you truly are evolving as a business you must make a decision to become the person who can let go of control.

You will evolve to the person who can allow goood people to join your TEAM and help you replicate. If you are one of those people who thinks NOBODY can do it as well as you that is more a representation of your own insecurities and EGO than anything. While there is truth in "nobody will work harder than you at your business" you CANNOT outwork 2 people.

Instead of thinking small and viewing output as 1 to 1 you must think with replication and a team. If you hire someone who can do at least 70% the job that is a WIN. This is where the law of replication comes in to SCALE. Say you have 2 people at 70% that's a 40% improvement in production alone.

Mistakes will happen. But you will also be able to generate momentum in your business as you grow that can make up for any lost revenue due to growing pains. Growing a team is more fulfilling and also allows you to do bigger jobs, get more reviews, seem more legit-imate in the marketplace. I believe you should always seek to replicate yourself and scale your business but do so when you have enough revenue to justify it! I was doing 30k a month solo before I ran out of steam. The next year we did 70k a month just duplicating our efforts! So if you build it they will come. Give your TEAM ownership and they will help you win!

Teamwork makes the DREAMWORK!

CHAPTER 21:
REPUTATION

How do you consistently grow your business and keep a pipeline full of loyal repeats and word of mouth? It's a lot easier than you think! Here are 5 things to do that will guarantee you build a strong reputation in your area.

1. **Google Reviews**- we automate our Google reviews by our CRM. Most people will google your company as a way of doing research to look at the reviews. If you don't have many or have a few bad ones (that happens and you can't prevent it) that will NEGATIVELY effect your reputation in your area.

2. **Facebook**- Get your business page as many reviews as you can. Make sure you are also actively sharing on your personal page and local groups that way you stay relevant to your community.

3. **Emails**-Make sure you keep an email list of all your customers. We send monthly emails to keep our customers educated on our business growth, contributions to the community, and current specials. This way you can systemetize your reputation by keeping your customers in the loop.

4. **Local Business Groups** - We are involved with in person networking to maintain a face to face reputation with local businesses via the Chamber of Commerce and other networking groups. Remember everything online is great but it's better to meet people as people!
5. **Flyers/Christmas Cards**-We send flyers seasonally and Christmas cards every year. This way we can stay in touch with our customers without trying to sell them.

Reputation boils down to how you treat your customers. Remeber you are in the service business and that means doing what is right even when it doesn't feel like the right thing to do. Doing "good" to a customer will amount to referrals and opportunities down the road. Remember at the end of the day our goal is to have the reputation of service! Reputation is all about staying in front of you customers and controlling how they view you! You can do the best job but if it's been 3 years since you did it they probably have forgotten about you. Your reputation is the most important part of business. Long after the quality of work is done people are going to remember you based upon how you made them feel. The entire process of your reputation starts when they first hear about you, the interaction leading to service, the quality of work and the customer follow up! Once you get your reputation you want to maintain it and keep it up consistently. That will allow your business to grow year over year without having to hunt new customers and losing your old ones due to not farming your past list.

CHAPTER 22:
WHERE DO YOU GO NOW?

Congratulations of getting through this book. We just touched the surface on how to go from 0 to your first 100k. Make sure f you haven't already check out our podcast **The Wash Bros Podcast** where we discuss exactly what we do to grow our businesses as well as talk about our mindsets, friendships and how we are evolving as business owners.

We are also putting together other books and courses that go deeper into the topics you have read here. This book is meant to give you a high level viewpoint of what we think is important to have a successful washing business. If you notice we didn't have a lot on equipment here because we believe the **business** is the most important part to your success.

Business is one of the most rewarding careers paths you can choose because it's an extension of you! The washing community is a great community full of endless opportunities of location, service specialty and seasons. We are passionate about the industry and that's why we are looking to connect and grow together.

WHERE DO YOU GO NOW?

"A dumb man learns from himself a smart man learns from others."

We all have something to contribute that can help each other grow into the best versions of ourselves and businesses. We look forward to having you in our community!

Listen to The Wash Bros Podcast

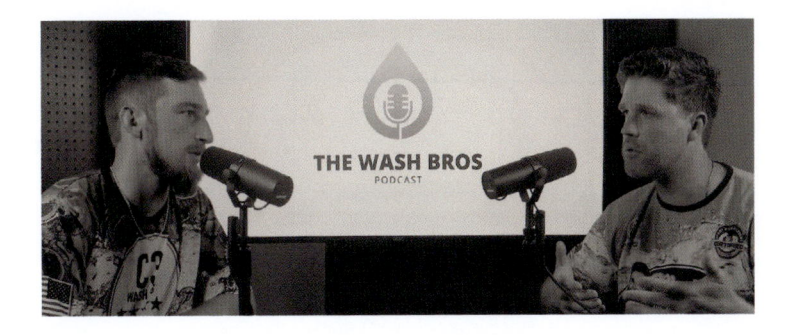

Follow us @ https://www.facebook.com/WASHBROSPODCAST

Subscribe on YouTube, iTunes and Spotify

Learn Everything You Need on PowerWashingCoach.com

Bonus Material

As a thank you for reading our book we want to give you some done for you templates to help you with your business. Marketing, Sales and SOPs!

Creating Your Mission Statement

MISSION:
"Set the standards for quality, professional, and reliable detailing services in our area"

VISION:
"Be an example for creating the ultimate work experience through having fun and achieving our goals"

CORE VALUES:					
Integrity	Honesty	Loyalty to the team	Family Culture	Selfless Service

BRAND POSITION / DIFFERENTIATORS:
System Oriented, Professional, Industry Experts, Trusted in the community, Look Good/Feel Good/Play

STRATEGIC OBJECTIVES:				
Daily Routine/Task lists READY TO ATTACK	Outline goals, SOPs, and training procedures	Create consistent sales process that works without Eric	Weekly team building meetings to enhance company culture	Engagement the community to GIVE BACK

KEY MARKET SEGMENTS - "WHERE WE'LL WIN"			
Commercial Accounts (hotels, gas stations, mgmt companies)	PROFESSIONAL interior cleaning services	High Income Suburbs	Commercial grade equipment

MAIN COMPETITIVE ADVANTAGES - "HOW WE'LL WIN"				
Disabled Veteran Status to win accounts	Team of Professional Staff	Branding and marketing	Referral Program	Giving Back

Here is an example of how to create your mission statement. Fill this out for your company on the next page!

Create Your Mission Statement Below

MISSION:

VISION:

CORE VALUES:

BRAND POSITION / DIFFERENTIATORS:

STRATEGIC OBJECTIVES:

KEY MARKET SEGMENTS - "WHERE WE'LL WIN"

MAIN COMPETITIVE ADVANTAGES - "HOW WE'LL WIN"

SWOT Analysis

A SWOT analysis is a compilation of your company's strengths, weaknesses, opportunities and threats. The primary objective of a SWOT analysis is to help organizations develop a full awareness of all the factors involved in making a business decision.

SWOT ANALYSIS

STRENGTHS	WEAKNESSES
Good market for growth	Too easy going. Not enough policy driven
Good core values	No current hiring process. Need more filtering criteria
Strong leader Empower employees, trained staff	Capacity issues. Grew too quickly
Staff hungry to grow Growth opportunities - pay raise schedules	
Flexible Schedules for employees	
Wife is great at admin	
Strong Cash position	

OPPORTUNITIES	THREATS
Need a better marketing strategy More consistent	Complacency
Need to keep good employees. Also hire more	Not thinking BIG enough
Commercial window cleaning growth	Employees leaving or not being consistent
	Not enough deal flow

Complete Your SWOT Analysis

SWOT ANALYSIS	
STRENGTHS	**WEAKNESSES**
OPPORTUNITIES	**THREATS**

How To Find Your Why

Here are the questions we recommend answering:

What inspired your business idea?
What's interesting about your founding story?
What is unique about your business?
What problem is your company trying to solve?
How has your business evolved?
What's your business purpose? Why does your company exist?
Is there a specific cause your business is supporting?
What do you believe in—personally and professionally?

The Golden Circle

What
Every organization on the planet knows WHAT they do. These are products they sell or the services.

How
Some organizations know HOW they do it. These are the things that make them special or set them apart from their competition.

Why
Very few organizations know WHY they do what they do. WHY is not about making money. That's a result. WHY is a purpose, cause or belief. It's the very reason your organization exists.

Personality Types

Take 16 personalities Test - www.16personalities.com

Since we are all different it is important to know ourselves and our employees based upon our personality matrix. The more we are aware of the different types of people out there and how to communicate effectively with them. The more success we have in selling, marketing and team building. This is a great resource to learn your personality type and that of others.

Another Great Test is the DISC Personality. You need to use the appropriate traits to correctly communicate with the personality type. By understanding the nature of the other person you can bridge the GAP and create a connection with them!

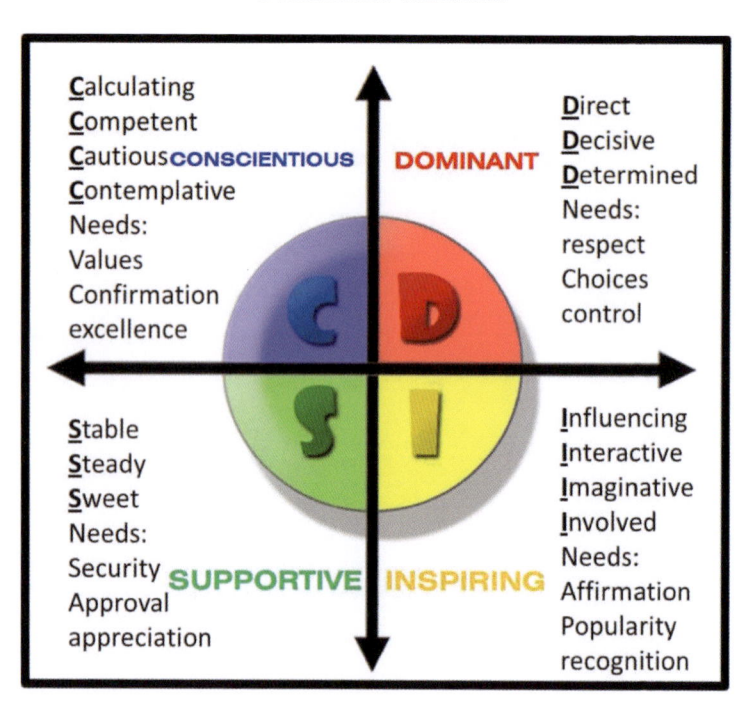

Calculating
Competent
Cautious CONSCIENTIOUS
Contemplative
Needs:
Values
Confirmation
excellence

DOMINANT

Direct
Decisive
Determined
Needs:
respect
Choices
control

Stable
Steady
Sweet
Needs:
Security   SUPPORTIVE   INSPIRING
Approval
appreciation

Influencing
Interactive
Imaginative
Involved
Needs:
Affirmation
Popularity
recognition

Sales 101

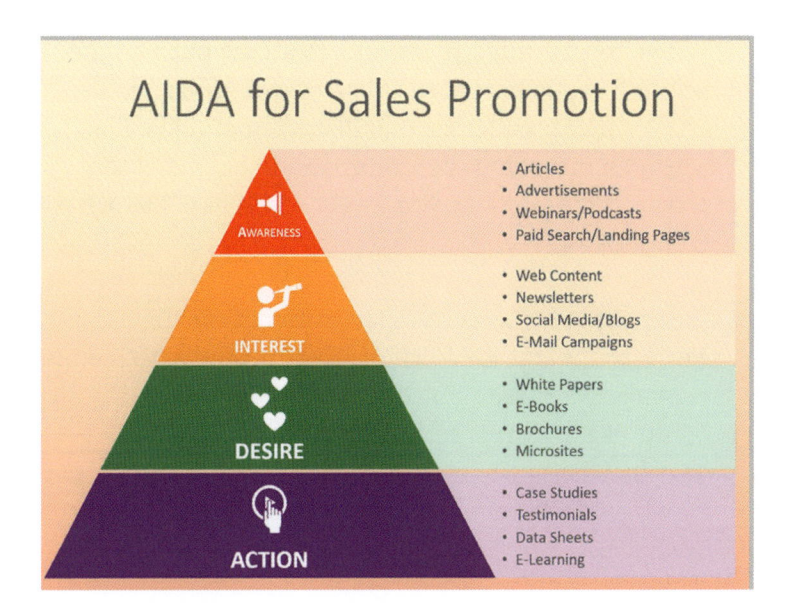

AIDA for Sales Promotion

Awareness
- Articles
- Advertisements
- Webinars/Podcasts
- Paid Search/Landing Pages

Interest
- Web Content
- Newsletters
- Social Media/Blogs
- E-Mail Campaigns

Desire
- White Papers
- E-Books
- Brochures
- Microsites

Action
- Case Studies
- Testimonials
- Data Sheets
- E-Learning

We use the AIDA framework to drive leads down the "funnel" to covert into sales.

Create a USP- What makes you DIFFERENT!

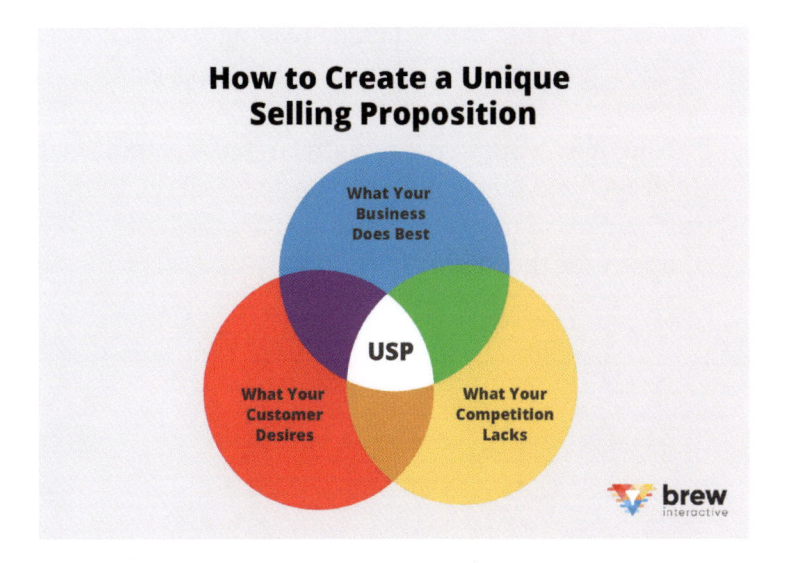

How to Create a Unique Selling Proposition

- What Your Business Does Best
- What Your Customer Desires
- What Your Competition Lacks

USP = intersection of all three

brew interactive

When you are advertising and creating your Unique Selling Proposition needs to be on your WHY and HOW you are different than the competitions. Don't worry about selling the features and benefits of the service but more why you as a company are the better fit than the rest.

I see people FAIL by trying to differentiate the TECHNICAL vs the WHY of their business. Remember people want a clean house and they want someone they know, like and trust to make that happen.

Don't get stuck selling "technobabble" and lose your prospect.

We sell with Emotion. It is very important that when we explain and sell our selves we don't use jargon or industry terminology that will create a disconnect with the prospect.

We want to speak at a 3rd grade reading level to create the most emotional experience for our prospects.

Instead of wowing someone with jargon to sound smart. Go deeper and relate to them on a deeper level. Gain trust and make them FEEL that you are the best company for the job.

Optimize Google My Business

1. Make Sure You Qualify For A Listing
2. Verify Your Business's Information
3. Add Your Business Name
4. Pick The Best Google Business Profile Categories To Describe Your Business
5. Use A Precise & Accurate Business Location
6. Add Service Areas For Your Service-Area Business
7. State Your Opening Hours
8. Provide A Phone Number
9. Provide A Business Website
10. Point Customers To Your Appointment URL
11. Google Business Profile Description
12. Add Products And Services
13. Google Business Profile Highlights And Attributes
14. Menu & Booking Items For Restaurants, Hotels & Bars
15. Take High-Resolution Photos And Videos
16. Enable The GBP Messaging Feature
17. Reply To Reviews
18. Write Posts And Updates Regularly
19. Showcase Your Opening Date
20. Take Advantage Of Google's Business Site

Basic Ad Copy Examples

Looking for 5 Star exterior cleaning ?
Here's what we offer at (Your Company) ⬇ ⬇ ⬇
- ☑ Pressure Washing
- ☑ Soft Washing
- ☑ House Washing
- ☑ Driveway Cleaning
- ☑ Roof Cleaning
- ☑ Residential & Commercial

Check us out on Google 5 Star   reviews!
Get Your Instant quote at (Your company.com)

Discover How to Easily Double Your Home's Curb Appeal with One Quick Little Trick For Only $69.

Think of all the time, effort, or money you spend on your lawn and garden to look its best. Now, consider that your driveway takes up half your front yard.

Moss, Grime, Dirt, Mud and Weeds Covering Your Driveways, Walkways, and Patios Look Messy and Dramatically Take Away From the Overall Clean and Desirable Look of Your Property.
Blast Away All That Unsightly Mess Today!

This Week's Driveway + Front Entrance Special

Only $69

For Less Than It Costs To Rent a Pressure Washer
You'll Save the Agony of Doing It Yourself

Book Now 778.434.2699

Call This Week! While We're In Your Neighbourhood.
Regular Price $99.

Give Us A Try!
We Guarantee
Complete Satisfaction!

Why Book With Us Today?

Get It Clean and Enjoy Today. Don't Wait Until Summer Is Over. We Clean Anytime, Rain or Shine

Who Wants to Pressure Wash on Their Day Off?

You Can't Even Rent a Pressure Washer for Our Special Price!

Save Yourself Time, a Sore back, Sore Hands, a Muddy Face, and Wet Clothes.

Pressure Washing is Not Fun.

Professional Knowledge and Equipment Guarantees to Blast Away All That Winter Has Left Behind.

$2 Million Insurance.

Worksafe BC Regulated.

Special "Early Bird" Gift to Monterra Residents

You've Won a Free Driveway Cleaning

Dear Monterra Resident,

I'm giving away Free Driveway Cleanings to Monterra Homeowners who respond to this letter before April 1, 2013.

Now, I don't give away free driveway cleaning to just anybody - I'd be out of business if I did that.

However, after doing 11 homes in Monterra, I've come to realize it is the perfect area to get more clients. In my experience, homeowners in Monterra are really looking to maintain and keep their home looking great and they appreciate having a long-term, "go-to" service they can trust and rely on.

Well, I'd like to be that service for you. And to prove it, I'd like to give you a free gift...

One Free Driveway Cleaning up to 600 sq ft

There is absolutely no-cost, no-obligation, not teeny tiny print. No strings attached. This will just give you and me a way to get to know each other. And you'll get to see, first-hand, how we take pride in delivering you amazing results.

We'll get rid of all the grime, gunk, and weeds that have built up over the years of wet winters and we'll save you hours of back breaking, clothes soaking, mud splashing labour.

Once your driveway is sparkling clean, if you like, I can measure out your remaining outdoor surfaces and discuss any other cleaning you may want done. But only if you choose.

These are great to model but don't copy verbatim. Remember to model this in your own voice.

Print Media Ideas

Printed in Great Britain
by Amazon